First Facts®

HOLIDAY SKETCHBOOK

A Halloween DRAWING Spooktacular!

CAPSTONE PRESS
a capstone imprint

by Jennifer M. Besel
illustrated by Lucy Makuc

First Facts are published by Capstone Press,
1710 Roe Crest Drive, North Mankato, Minnesota 56003
www.capstonepub.com

Library of Congress Cataloging-in-Publication Data
Besel, Jennifer M.
 A Halloween drawing spooktacular! / by Jennifer M. Besel ; illustrated by Lucy Makuc.
   pages cm.—(First facts. Holiday sketchbook)
 Includes bibliographical references and index.
 Summary: "Step-by-step instructions and sketches show how to draw common Halloween images
and symbols"—Provided by publisher.
 ISBN 978-1-4765-3091-8 (library binding)
 ISBN 978-1-4765-3446-6 (pbk.)
 ISBN 978-1-4765-3422-0 (ebook pdf)
1. Halloween in art—Juvenile literature. 2. Drawing—Technique—Juvenile literature. I. Makuc, Lucy.
II. Title.
NC825.H32B47 2014
743'.87—dc23   2013002368

Editorial Credits
Juliette Peters, designer; Kathy McColley, production specialist

Photo Credits
Capstone Studio: Karon Dubke, 5 (photos); Shutterstock: Azuzl (design element), Kalenik Hannah
(design element), oculo (design element)

Printed in the United States of America in North Mankato, Minnesota.
032013   007223CGF13

Table of Contents

Color Me Scared............................ 4

Eye See You 6

Goo-o'-Lantern 8

Going Batty 10

All Wrapped Up 12

Catitude 14

Mr. Monster................................ 16

Fanged Friend 18

Under a Spell 20

Dancing Bones 22

Read More.................................... 24

Internet Sites 24

Color Me Scared

Snakes and toads
and witches brew.
Halloween is fun,
and learning to draw is too!

Don't be scared if you don't know where to begin. This book is just for you. Follow these tips and the simple steps on each page. You'll be drawing creepy, crawly creatures in no time.

 TIP 1 **Draw lightly.** You will need to erase some lines as you go, so draw them light.

 TIP 2 **Add details.** Little details, such as cobwebs or eyes, make your drawings super scary.

 TIP 3 **Color your drawings.** Color can make a creepy drawing even scarier!

You won't need a broom or a full moon.
But you will need some supplies.

drawing paper

eraser

pencil

colored pencils
or markers

pencil sharpener

Sharpen your pencils, and get ready to draw all the
sights of Halloween. It will be a spooktacular time!

Eye See You

Spiders and eyeballs are Halloween favorites. Put them together to create a very creepy creature.

Final

Don't Forget!
Erase lines that go under something else. For example, erase the lines that go through the eye circles in step 2.

1 Draw an oval for the body. Overlap the oval with a smaller oval for the head.

2 Draw two circles for eyes centered on the head. Draw three more circles along the top of the head.

3 Draw eight squiggly lines around the body for legs. Add small circles inside the eyes for pupils.

4 Round out each leg. Add eye details. Then give the spider small fangs.

Goo-o'-Lantern

Nothing is more gross than goo and guts.
Draw a pumpkin's gooey brains for an extra
Halloween scare.

Final

1

Draw a large circle. Draw two circle eyes, a triangle nose, and a half circle mouth.

2

Add detail lines to the eyes, nose, and mouth. Draw a scalloped line near the top of the circle. Add squiggly lines like a cloud along the line to look like goop.

3

Draw a small oval inside the large circle and above the scalloped line. Add detail lines to make the top look like a lid. Draw a handle on top. Then add detail lines along the bottom.

4

Draw teeth inside the mouth. Erase the lines where the mouth meets the teeth. Add a curly line to the handle. Also add detail lines to the lid. Draw seeds in the goop and in the eyes.

Going Batty

Fly through this drawing like a bat flies through the night. Its little smile will make people wonder what it's been up to.

Final

1

Draw an oval for the body. Overlap the oval with a circle for the head. Draw two long ovals for feet. Add straight lines for wings and curved lines for ears.

2

Connect the straight wing lines with scalloped lines. Add detail lines to the ears. Then give your bat eyes and a smile.

3

Draw larger circles around the eyes. Add a half circle inside the body.

4

Widen the wing lines. Then turn the half circle on the body into a scalloped spot of fur. Finally, add fangs to the bat's mouth and small lines for a nose.

All Wrapped Up

Stories say a curse brings mummies to life. But a pencil and your imagination can bring one to life too.

Final

1

Draw an oval for the body. Overlap the body with an oval with a straight bottom for the head. Draw straight lines for the legs and arms. Use curved lines for feet.

2

Round out each arm and leg. Make the hands look like mittens and the feet like socks.

3

Draw two circles on the head for eyes. Add two smaller circles inside them as pupils. Draw a thin line for a mouth, and add a tongue hanging out. Add a thumb to the hand in front.

4

Draw lines all over the mummy to look like bandages.

Catitude

Cats only do what they want to do. Let that attitude shine through on this Halloween kitty.

Final

1

Draw a mushroom top for a head. Draw a circle under the head and a larger circle below and to the right of the first. Draw straight lines around the circles to start the body.

2

Draw straight lines off the head to start the ears. Draw a curvy line for a tail. Draw lines inside the body shape to look like front and back legs.

3

Round out the ears and tail. Add eyes and a nose. Erase the circles inside the cat's body.

4

Draw jagged lines to create fur on the head, tail, and back. Add a straight line from the nose to the bottom line of the head.

Mr. Monster

He growls. He howls.
He stomps. He clomps.
Draw this silly monster
to scare away the other
monsters under your bed!

Final

1

Draw a rectangle for the upper body. Overlap a half circle over the rectangle for a head. Add arms and curved legs. Draw a straight line on the half circle as a forehead.

2

Draw a scalloped line on the head as hair. Add circles for ears, eyes, and fingers. Add straight lines over the eyes. Draw a jagged line on the bottom of the shirt. Then draw shoes.

3

Draw a curved line at the top of the head. Add details to the eyes and ears. Add a nose and mouth. Draw a curved line from the monster's jaw to the shirt bottom on one side. Repeat on the other side to make a vest. Draw a square on his knee and an oval inside the left shoe.

4

Draw small buttons coming from the monster's neck. Add line details to the forehead and knee square to look like they've been sewn. Finish by adding line details to the vest and shirt.

Fanged Friend

It's not Halloween without a sneaky vampire. Draw him near a bedroom window to give your friends or family nightmares.

Final

1 Draw a rounded heart for a head. Next draw a square body under the head and two small rectangle arms. Draw simple hands too. Add pants at the bottom and half circles at the neck.

2 Draw pointy ears on each side of the head. Give the creature a bow tie, shoes, and the start of a cape. Draw thumbs on the hands. Then curve the bottom of the shirt.

3 Give the creature circle eyes, a half circle nose, and a thin mouth and eyebrows. Add a curved line above the head for hair. Draw the side parts of the cape. Then give his shoes little heels.

4 Add larger circles around the eyes and fangs to the mouth. Finish the shirt with a line down the middle and three buttons. Finally, add detail lines to the ears and sleeves, and draw a scalloped line to finish the bottom of the cape.

Under a Spell

You won't need a potion to make Halloween magic. This little witch should do the trick.

1

Draw a long, thin oval for a hat brim. Add a curved triangle to the top of the oval. Draw an oval face under the hat. Then draw a larger oval body down and to the left of the face. Add an upside down "C" going through and around the body.

2

Draw scalloped lines for hair around the face. Add a rectangle arm on the right side of the body. Draw a long, thin oval for the witch to sit on. Add two circles and a rectangle at the end of the oval. Then give her little feet.

3

Draw a simple hand around the broomstick. Draw curved and jagged lines on the end of the broom. Finish her feet to look like boots.

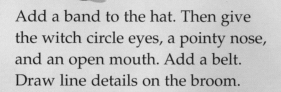

4

Add a band to the hat. Then give the witch circle eyes, a pointy nose, and an open mouth. Add a belt. Draw line details on the broom.

5

Add buckles to the belt and hat band. Put teeth in the witch's mouth. Draw half circles around the eyes to make them open wide.

Final

Dancing Bones

This crazy character feels the music in his bones.
Feel free to "dress" him up with a bow tie or hat.

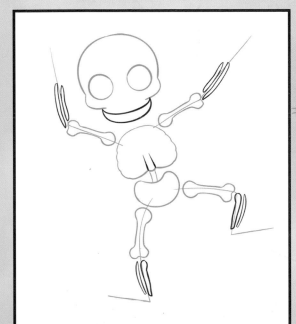

1 Draw a circle head. Draw a half circle under the head. Draw a smaller half circle upside down under the first. Draw thin lines for the arms and legs.

2 Add eyes and cheeks to the head. Draw two short lines between the half circles. Then draw bone shapes around the thin arm and leg lines.

3 Add a jaw to the head. Draw skinny bones after the arm and leg bones. Then add two small lines in the upper body to start the rib cage.

4

Draw small circles after the arm and leg bones. Add a small circle neck. Draw small circles for feet. Also give the character a nose.

5

Use curved lines for eyebrows and ribs. Add small circles to the feet and the lower half circle. Use small lines to add details to the mouth. Then add fingers.

Final

Read More

Besel, Jennifer M. *A Thanksgiving Drawing Feast*. Holiday Sketchbook. North Mankato, Minn.: Capstone Press, 2014.

Goldsworthy, Kaite. *Halloween*. Celebrating American Holidays. New York: AV2 by Weigl, 2012.

Masiello, Ralph. *Ralph Masiello's Halloween Drawing Book*. Watertown, Mass.: Charlesbridge, 2012.

Internet Sites

FactHound offers a safe, fun way to find Internet sites related to this book. All of the sites on FactHound have been researched by our staff.

Here's all you do:

Visit *www.facthound.com*

Type in this code: 9781476530918

Super-cool stuff!

Check out projects, games and lots more at
www.capstonekids.com